No More Mild Mannered Business

Simple Ways To Move Your Business
From Good To Great

by **Fernando Camacho**

Copyright © 2019 FJC Enterprises

All rights reserved

ISBN 978-1-7320635-1-8

To all my fellow entrepreneurs who are working your butts off to make your dreams a reality.

Table of Contents

Introduction 1

1 - 80/20ing Your Business 7

2 - Redefining The Customer Experience................. 21

3 - Survey Says 35

4 - Magical Business Lessons From Disney 49

5 - Stealing Customers From Your Competition 67

6 - Dealing with Dick 75

7 - The Dangers of Bad Customers Service.............. 83

8 - Organic vs. Paid... 97

In Closing 105

Introduction

I'm very happy and grateful that this book has found it's way into your hands - and I hope that you'll feel the same, once you're done reading it.

Let's start off with a quick question: Do you want an average business?

Seems like a pretty dumb thing to ask - I mean who starts a business just to be average. I'm guessing you don't believe that average is good enough. I bet you want to make an exceptional business that has raving fans instead of customers and is talked about as one of the best in your industry.

The problem is that so many people *say* they want an exceptional business but are doing very

Introduction

average things (which is delivering average results) with their business. If you're not very intentional about what you do you will typically default to the industry norm - which is the average, and average sucks. Average doesn't really pay the bills. Average will not make you thrilled to jump out of bed to go to work. Average will not keep your business around long term.

When you get stuck in an average business you end up with in what I call a "mild mannered" business. Think of Clark Kent, Superman's alter ego. If you've ever watched any of the Superman movies, you've seen Clark Kent awkwardly existing in the background, often ignored and always passed over. He's just an average guy, no one to take notice of. Superman wants it like that because he doesn't want anyone to know that it's him. That way he can live among us humans, see where the trouble is and swoop in to save the day.

There's nothing more frustrating to me then when some bad guy starts messing with Lois Lane and I have to sit and watch mild mannered Clark Kent just sit there and do nothing. I mean, that's Supreman! I want him to just rip off that suit right then and there and save the day. But he doesn't. He can't. Clark has to keep up the facade and hide the fact that he's really Superman.

I see so many hard working people that truly have an amazing product or service but are stuck operating in as mild mannered businesses because they don't understand how to put on the cape and fly. They just don't know the key things they can do to break out of averagetown and take everything they do to the next level – which comes with more success, more customers, more appreciation and more money.

After a decade or two of working for other people, I finally figured out that I just wasn't cut out for being an employee. Now, there's nothing wrong with being a part of a great company and working for someone else, I just finally understand my own personal internal make up and know that I'm happiest when I'm in complete control of everything, making all the decisions, taking all the risks, wearing all the hats, responsible for all the success, as well as all the failures (and I've had quite a few).

Since discovering that I'm an entrepreneur at heart I've started and run a number of businesses:

Introduction

dog training, online courses, membership sites, e-commerce store, speaking, consulting and most recently, a Facebook/Instagram advertising agency. As you can see, I've dabbled in a lot of different things, which has forced me to get educated in a lot of different areas and done all kinds of experimentation and trial and error. I would love to tell you that all those businesses were runaway successes, but that's not the truth. Some did very well, some not so much.

Whether they succeeded or failed they all taught me some valuable lessons that have improved all my future efforts. That, combined with being able to work with a number of different businesses in my consulting business, as well as my digital agency, has allowed me to see first hand what works and what typically leads to businesses closing their doors.

In addition, I'm a crazy reader who goes through a few books every month – all of which focus on self improvement and business development. I love to learn what other people have done, soak up their experiences and implement things that have worked into my own life and business.

This book covers a number of the ideas that I've used in my businesses and with my clients that have had huge positive ripple effects. I'm not pretending to be some guru that has seen it all and knows it all. On the contrary, I'm just a semi-normal guy looking to share what I've learned over the course of my business life.

My hope is that one or more of these points will resonate with you and you'll take the necessary action to implement it into your business and enjoy all the success you deserve. The book is intentionally short – I know you're busy and that you've got a lot of things on your to-do list. It shouldn't take you long to go through these pages, but don't forget to make a plan to take action on what you read here. Reading great ideas and doing nothing about them is the same as never learning them. You must take action.

Alright, let's get this party started . . .

1

80/20ing Your Business

Do you constantly feel like you're running around like a Jack Russell who just downed a double espresso? Are you crazy busy every day but always leave feeling like you didn't really accomplish anything?

It's a frustrating feeling and one I've felt quite a lot in the past. When your business is like this, you keep spinning your wheels but never move forward. This is where a lot of people experience burnout and breakdowns.

The problem isn't that you're not working hard enough, it's that **you're probably focusing on the wrong things**. It's true. You're most likely running yourself ragged on stuff that seems pressing but is not and are exhausting yourself because your efforts are in the wrong place.

It's time you started to streamline your input to maximize your output and the best way to do that is to use the 80/20 principal.

What is 80/20?

It all started way back in 1906 when economist, Vilfredo Pareto observed that 80% of income in Italy was received by 20% of the Italian population. After further study it became apparent that for many events, roughly 80% of the effects come from 20% of the causes. Soon people were seeing 80/20 everywhere. The assumption is that most of the results in any situation are determined by a small number of causes.

Once you start looking at your life, you'll notice that there is an 80/20 present in almost every single thing you do.

Here are some examples of 80/20 in action:

- If you have 10 rooms in your house, you spend 80% of your time in 2 of them (20%)

- If you have 50 different apps on your phone, 80% of your time is spent on just 10 of them (20%)
- 80% of your happiness with your spouse is a result of only 20% of what you do with them
- 80% of your social activities are with only 20% of your friends and family

And on and on and on – 80/20 is everywhere.

What It Means For You In Your Business

- 80% of your business comes from 20% of your customers
- 80% of your problems come from 20% of the causes
- 80% of your revenue comes from 20% of your services
- 80% of your new customers come from 20% of your marketing
- 80% of complaints come from 20% of your customers
- 80% of your business effectiveness comes from 20% of your staff

As you can see, there is an 80/20 in just about everything.

Too many businesses are wasting time, effort and money on the other 80% of stuff that isn't moving the needle on their success. They are focusing on busy work and issues that seem pressing but is not what's going to have the biggest impact when you look at the big picture.

You need to determine what your 20% is in every aspect of your business.

Making 80/20 Work For You

1. You need to focus on your company's top clients.

Yes, every customer should be taken care of but they are definitely not all equally important. Some clients are exceptional. These are the ones who do lots of repeat business, are reliable and easy to work with. These guys bring you the most money and need to be treated special.

You should pay close attention to them, making sure they are happy and well cared for. You also can grow your business by adapting your services to meet their needs. Find out what more you can do for them, what other services they would like and how you can increase their bond with you and your company.

2. Get rid of the 20% of customers that are causing you the most grief and are causing you the most problems.

These people are like a virus in your business and will eat away your time, test your patience and aggravate your staff. They are taking away resources that could be spent on good customers who will appreciate what you do and bring you more money.

Think of your customer base like a rose bush. When some of the roses turn brown and wilt on a rose bush, a good gardener doesn't spend his time on them trying to bring them back to life. No way. He just cuts them off. He does this because he understands that by getting rid of the bad roses, it leaves more resources for the good buds. Getting rid of the bad flowers makes the rose bush stronger and more beautiful in the long run.

Take a look at your customers and do some pruning.

3. Figure out who the top 20% of your staff is and make sure you take real good care of them.

Look at your organization and find your top performers. You probably already know who they are. They're the ones who are the most effective, helpful and skilled at their job. They don't cause trouble and are very trustworthy and loyal.

Once you have your list, find ways to reward them. It could be a $10 Starbucks gift card, an extra paid day off or even just some verbal appreciation (that goes way farther than you realize). Don't make a big fuss in front of your other employees (that will just cause problems) but acknowledge their strong performance privately and let them know how much you appreciate them.

4. Determine where you are getting most of your new customers from and then double down on those marketing channels.

You'll find that 80% of new customers are coming from only 20% of sources. Figure out which advertising and promotional techniques are working well and do more of them. There's no reason to try every new thing that comes along. Look at what's already working and just amplify it.

5. Look at the services you offer and find the one or ones that are responsible for 80% of your revenue and focus on them.

There's no need to offer a gazillion different services. It's usually better to stick to a few core ones and make them more awesome. Having too many service offerings dilutes your resources and can often confuse your clients (too many choices makes people uncomfortable and can lead to them choosing nothing).

When Apple brought back Steve Jobs they were in big financial trouble, but under Job's leadership, Apple exceeded all past success. The first thing Job's did was cancel 70% of the products Apple was offering and just focus on a few. That decision allowed Apple to concentrate all its efforts on making those core products amazing.

Pick your core services and work to improve them every year.

6. Look at the things you do every single day. I bet you'll see that most (about 80%) of your business success is driven by only 20% of what you do daily.

Stop focusing on stuff that doesn't matter. Delegate as much as you can to others or just stop doing it altogether. You will be surprised at how unnecessary much of what you do is and how little it affects your long term success.

I've done this constantly over the years. I started out blogging, then I discovered podcasting, then got into making videos and then started teaching on webinars. Now, I could do them all - but should I?

No, no, no.

I did an 80/20 and realized what was giving me the biggest results in my business was webinars. So, you'll notice I don't blog, podcast or do videos as much anymore, but webinars are a regular part of my business because they bring in the most money.

Look at the things you do and figure out what you can trim and make sure you're focusing on the few things that move your business farther, faster.

Your "Three Lists Of Freedom"

To help you figure this out, I invite you to do an exercise one of my old business coaches, Chris

Ducker, had me do. He calls it, "The Three Lists To Freedom."

On the next page you'll find three columns. In the first column I want you to list all the things you just hate to do. The second column is for all the things you can't do yourself – things that are a struggle or you don't quite have the skills to do. Lastly, in the third column put down all the things you shouldn't be doing. This is a hard one because you may like doing some of this stuff, but in reality your time would be better spent elsewhere.

All the tasks you've listed here are the things you should work to get off of your plate. Find ways to delegate, train someone else to do them, or outsource. Once you are free of these tasks you'll be left to focus on what you're really supposed to be doing; the stuff that will drive your business and help you enjoy the ride.

When you're working on utilizing 80/20 in your life and business, you'll see that it's often easy to grab hold of the 20% but it can be quite hard sometimes to let go of that 80%.

Figuring Your 20%

In his book, *80/20 Sales And Marketing* , Perry Marshall tells a story of a young 17 year old who went to Las Vegas to become a professional poker player. Quickly, this kid realized he needed help and found a mentor – a veteran poker player who agreed to take him under his wing.

No More Mild Mannered Business

The first lesson he needed to teach his young protégé was to only play games you can win. To do this, he brought him to a local strip club. Hard rock was pounding through the speakers as half naked women snaked around the stages while the alcohol numbed crowd watched.

The mentor pulled out a shotgun, slipped it under the table, popped the chamber open and snapped it quickly shut, making that signature "cha-chick" sound (what gun enthusiasts call "racking the shotgun").

Immediately a few heads (about 20% of the crowd) spun around, trying to figure out where the sound came from. The wise poker mentor looked over at his wide-eyed friend and said, "Never play poker with those guys. Your job is to play with everyone else."

By racking the shotgun, he was able to see which guys are very aware and not to be messed with because they understand exactly what that sound was. Your job is to "rack the shotgun" in all the things that you do so you can figure out the 80/20 of any situation.

When you have a live event at your location (maybe a holiday party), the people that show up are the customers who are most likely to be loyal and give you repeat business. That's your 20%.

If you post something on social media, the people who leave a comment or share it are the 20% most likely to convert to a paying customer.

If you ask your staff to let you know how you can improve your business, the few that actually take the time to talk to you about it are your top 20%.

There are always ways to rack the shotgun. You just need to figure out how to do it in each situation and zero in on your 20%.

Taking It To The Next Level – 80/20ing The 80/20

It doesn't stop at 80/20 though. We can take it up a notch to really see where the cream of the crop is.

The Pareto Principle can be applied to itself. We already know that 20% of your customers represent 80% of your revenues. What Marshall found is that, within that initial 20%, the 80/20 rule also exists. Meaning that the top 20% of the top 20% of your customers represent 64% of your sales. **So the top 4% of your customers account for 64% of your sales.**

So if you just determine who the top 4% of your customers are and take great care of them, they will drive 64% of your yearly income. Pretty cool, huh?

ACTION PLAN

Find your 80/20 in all important aspects of your business.

CUSTOMERS - Find out which customers are spending the most money, reward them and then try to find people just like that.

MARKETING - Make sure you have metrics on all of your marketing efforts (this is why Facebook ads are great but coupon books and flyers suck) and only put money into the top 20% performers.

STAFF – Fire the bottom 10% of your employees. Reward your top achievers.

YOUR TIME – Delegate things you should not be doing – you shouldn't try to do it all – leverage your time, doing mostly the 20% of stuff that will make the biggest impact on your business.

Redefining The Customer Experience

As I've done more and more consulting with small businesses, I've noticed something that is a major, common problem. Most companies have their priorities all mixed up and put their emphasis on the wrong things. And this mishap is messing up their entire business, causing them unnecessary stress, while costing them both money and customers.

Most companies put all their focus, time and resources on sales and marketing.

Think about it.

How much education have you spent on sales and marketing?

How much money have you invested in your company's sales and marketing efforts?

How much of your on and offline resources is spent on getting more customers?

Now, how much time, money and resources do you put toward making your customers crazy happy?

Be honest. Actually, take out a piece of paper and quickly jot down all the things you do to get new customers. That includes what's on your website, paid advertising, social media posting, promotions, giveaways, networking, cross promotions, sales, etc.

Then, take out another piece of paper and write down all the things you do for your existing customers. How much money and time do you invest? What do you give them? How do you take care of them and make them feel special?

Once you do this, you should see right there, in black and white, the glaring difference between the two. If you're like most businesses, you'll see the sales and marketing side far exceed the customer care page.

No More Mild Mannered Business

This problem is something I've recently done a lot of research on and have been really thinking about lately. I do a lot of reading on successful people and businesses, and just finished two really good books which highlighted the very important principal of taking amazing care of your customers and spending more time and money on them, rather than on getting new ones.

The first book I read was *"The Everything Store: Jeff Bezos and the Age of Amazon"* by Brad Stone, which tells how Amazon.com got started, their struggle to stay in business and how they became one of the biggest companies in the world. It's a really interesting story, with lots of ups and downs and really shows what's possible if you have the right vision, perseverance and attitude. Jeff Bezos overcame tremendous obstacles and countless failures on his quest to revolutionize retail shopping forever.

The book taught me three really big lessons. One, if you really believe in something, don't let anyone talk you out of it. Two, never work for Amazon.com – Jeff is a brilliant guy but a tough person to work for. Three, if you always keep the customer in mind and strive to make their experience amazing, they will come back again and again.

Bezos was obsessed with the customer experience over everything else. There were countless times when he could have saved millions of dollars doing things differently, but if there was even a possibility of it negatively affecting the customer's experience in any way, Bezos didn't flinch at the money. He has a really good talent of thinking "big picture" and understanding that the better the customers felt, the more successful the company would be.

The customer was so important to Bezos that whenever they had a meeting at Amazon, he insisted that they always left an empty chair at the table to represent the customer. That empty chair would always remind them to keep the customer's interest in mind while they were making decisions or deciding on projects to take on. If it didn't benefit the customer in some way, it wouldn't go through.

This mindset is so important to keep in mind while you're growing your business. Often, people will cut corners or add policies without thinking about what it means to the customer and how it will make them feel. You should be constantly striving to remove friction for your customers and make their experience with your company easy, pleasurable and rewarding at every turn.

When Amazon first started selling toys, they were horribly unprepared for the Christmas rush. But Bezos had people working round the clock, buying products from brick and mortar stores and personally packaging boxes to make sure the customers got what they wanted in time for the holidays. This was done at great expense to Amazon, but the customers were happy, which is all that mattered to Bezos. This meant Amazon had to go deep into debt during these times and many analysts reported it would be their undoing. However, all those happy customers came back again and again, giving Amazon even more money over time and eventually making it extremely profitable.

It always comes down to the lifetime value of the customer. When you're operating on a sales and marketing mentality, you only see the initial sale - which isn't all that important. To make your business wildly successful, you need to get that first sale - but then you have to pour on the juice.

So the big question I have for you is, do you really know what it's like being your customer?

Do you know how they feel? What emotions come with dropping their dog off with you?

Most people will tell me they do, but have never actually experienced it, so they can never know for sure. I recommend conducting some surveys where you ask some specific questions about how they feel in each area of your services. You want to find out what their emotions are about every step in your business process - the more detailed the better.

If you can improve their emotional feeling as they do business with you, you'll be on your way to creating an experience instead of just a transaction.

Never Lose A Customer Again

The second book I just finished was *"Never Lose A Customer Again: Turn Any Sale Into Lifelong Loyalty In 100 Days"* by Joey Coleman. I highly recommend you give this one a read. You'll learn the eight phases of the customer experience and get some great examples of how to really wow your customers so that they have an amazing experience dealing with your company, every step of the way.

These steps begin with the potential customer deciding if they want to do business with you (the Asses phase) and ends with them becoming a raving fan who's telling everyone how awesome you are (the Advocate phase). As you may remember, I'm very focused on turning all my customers into raving fans. If you're able to do that, you create a referral machine that brings a steady flow of new customers into your business without you having to do any sales or marketing whatsoever.

The eight phases take you through the entire life cycle of your customer and details how you should craft their experience to be. Many mistaken businesses have so much hype and momentum built into the pre-sale phase and only a slight spark immediately, post-sale and just about nothing as time goes on. All the attention and effort is put into the very beginning, but those customers who have been with you for years eventually get forgotten as you work to bring in new faces.

Every single step in the life cycle of your customer is important and is worthy of improving.

Customer Experience Exercise

Let's do some role playing, shall we?

I want you to imagine that you are on the other side of your business. Pretend you are a brand new customer who's just given up your credit card, and now have to let go of your precious little fur baby for a day of daycare or week of boarding (I would do this for each service you provide), or whatever. How do you think you would feel? Nervous? Unsure? Not sure if you made the right decision?

Don't focus on what happens physically, try to experience the emotions you would be feeling. Then, think of all the things that someone could do at that moment to make you feel a little more comfortable. What would it take?

I've been on both sides of the transaction at dog daycare, and I can tell you what would make the difference for me. Having someone carefully and caringly lay out exactly what was going to happen; what the step-by-step process would be for my dog while staying there, would make me feel better. The sad reality is that most of the time, someone just takes the leash and says, "Thanks, pick him up in a couple of hours," then disappears with my dog.

Then, if it were my dog daycare, I would send that person a text in about 30 minutes with an update on how their dog was doing. That first visit is very nerve-racking for new pet parents, but I don't see any daycares understanding and doing something about that. Sad, because it's so simple and would GREATLY improve the customer experience at that critical early stage.

Next, imagine you're a regular daycare customer who's been there for six months. What's that experience like? Basically, I want you to go through every point in your customer life cycle and figure out some ways to improve their experience. Most of the time, the things that have the biggest affect will be the little, inexpensive touches that just shows you care about them.

Never ever take your customers or the customer experience for granted. The better you can make the process of doing business with you, the more business you'll get, period.

Here's another idea that can cause positive shock waves in your business. Every month, pick one or two customers and send them something cool in the mail. It could be a new dog toy or treats or a gift certificate for a pizza place. Just something unexpected that will leave them smiling. Unexpected surprises delight people and will strengthen the bond they have with you and your company that will be next to impossible to break.

Pro Tip: Look at their Twitter feed, Facebook wall and Instagram posts. See what they're doing, what they like and what they might need. Then, send them something personal just for them. I learned this from media influencer, Gary Vaynerchuk, who used to run his family's liquor store in New Jersey.

He tells a story of how a guy bought about $117 worth of crappy wine online from his store. On the surface, not a high value customer, but Gary Vee decided to give him an amazing experience. He looked over his Twitter feed and saw that he was a huge fan of the Chicago Bears football team, especially Jay Cutler, who was their quarterback at the time. He then went over to EBay and bought a jersey signed by Jay Cutler for about $350 and had it sent to him with a note that said, "Thank you so much for your order." Three or four weeks go by and nothing happens - no response from the guy at all. Then one day, an order comes in from a different guy who buys $4,800 of high end booze with a note that says, "My friend told me about you and he told me the story of the jersey you sent him . . ."

Pretty damn cool. If you want to hear Gary Vee tell that story (with more details), you can watch it here: *http://bit.ly/garyvee14*

What that shows is that you really care enough to go out of your way for them. If they feel that, you've got a raving fan for life.

Let's say I owned a dog daycare, here's something I would do. I would pick a customer every month or so (I would probably start with my best customers), and send them a custom stuffed animal that looked like their dog. There are a number of online places that do that and it costs about $199.

Can you imagine how that would make you feel to get that kind of gift unexpectedly? You would be blown away (and post it all over the internet).

The bottom line is that there is nothing more important than the experience you are giving your customers. Mess it up and nothing can save you. It doesn't matter if you have a high-end, state-of-the-art facility or are in the best location on the planet, a poor customer experience will kill you every time. Conversely, amazing customer experiences can overpower just about any other variable.

Be very intentional about the journey you take your customer on and continually look for ways to make it easier and more enjoyable.

Now go create something memorable for your customers.

ACTION PLAN

Take 10 - 20 minutes and write down what you currently do for your customers to take amazing care of them and keep them forever loyal. Then write down what you're going to do, knowing now just how important it is to show your current customers constant love, from this day forward.

3

Survey Says...

How good is your company?

How good are the services that you provide?

You know, as business owners, we think we know our business very well. We think we know what everybody wants; the best way to serve them, the best way to take care of our customers, the best way to over-deliver to them. We know the very best ways to take care of them.

We *think* we know that, but how do we really *know* that?

This is a trap that too many people fall into. We're convinced that what we think is what our customer base thinks. We understand them better than they understand themselves, so we know what's best for them and we're going to give them what we know they need.

<u>That is a huge, huge mistake</u> because what you think your customers value - what you think they care about - they may actually have no interest in. Maybe the things that you were undervaluing are what they really care about.

Finding out what your customers really value and then making sure you're facilitating that value is the big leverage point in your business. Even if you've got a great company that's providing amazing service, you should still always be trying to improve things. You should be continually finding out the real answers to those magic questions about your business.

What do my customers value? How do I make sure I deliver that value better?

Often this means taking some aspect of your business that is working well and making it even better. One of my entrepreneurial heroes, Walt Disney (more about Disney in the next chapter) was always doing this and that's why the Disney brand is the global success it is.

Walt was known to always keep "plussing" everything. He was never satisfied with just being good – he was always looking to constantly improve things. When they finished an animated movie that was the most amazing thing they ever created, Walt would ask, "Okay, now how do we plus it?"

This is the stuff that new businesses should be doing. These are questions that existing businesses should be asking. Businesses that are struggling and businesses that are thriving should always be asking, how good is our company? How good are the services that we provide?

You've got to ask those questions constantly so you can see exactly where you can improve. What areas do you need to do a little bit better in? What part of your business would most benefit from an upgrade?

The answers to these questions are the difference between an average business that's just breaking even and businesses that are exploding - doing so great and have so much momentum.

Now we need to figure out how to get the answers to these questions, and as you could probably guess, it's not from yourself and it's not from your staff. **Only your customers know exactly what is great about your company and where the weak points are.**

So ask them.

Ask your customers exactly what they like, what they don't like, and how you can improve everything about your business every single year. Even if everything is going great and you're having your best year ever, that's awesome, but how do you take it up another level this year?

Hopefully I've convinced you that you need to be asking your customers about your services. Now the question is, how should you ask them?

Should you just ask people as they come in and say, "Hey, how do you like what we do?" Or, "what do you like about our business? Do you like this? Do you not like this?"

That's a bad idea because you're putting people on the spot. You want to make it easy for them and the best way to do that is to create a simple survey on how your company is doing so you can get peoples' honest opinions about what's going on so you know the directions that you need to take in your business.

HOW TO DO IT

There are only a few things you need to do to make sure your survey is successful and will give you useful info you can take action on.

Number one, you want to make it anonymous. You will get **MUCH** better results if your customers know that you won't know it came from them.

Confronting them in-person, on the phone or even in an email really isn't good because they may still feel inhibited because you know who they are. They may like you and your staff and be afraid to hurt your feelings by telling you that some parts of your business could be better.

Instead you want to create a situation where they can be completely honest with you. Making it a blind survey where you don't know who filled it out will give them the comfort of being anonymous, allowing them to tell you exactly how they feel because they know it's never going to get traced back to them.

Number two, you have to make it easy for them.

Everyone's busy and everyone's got their own stuff to deal with. As much as your customers love you, they are more invested in their own lives than in yours. So the more difficult you make your survey process, the more hoops you make them jump through, the more time it takes them and the less likely they're going to do it. You want to make it super simple and super easy for them to accomplish. The less steps, the better, the less friction in the whole process, the more likely they are going to take the time to fill it out.

Luckily there's an online tool that makes creating a survey crazy easy. It's called Survey Monkey (www.surveymonkey.com). Best of all, it's free for up to 10 questions.

You can customize your survey and then create a link to email to your customer list. You don't want to post it on social media or to the general public because you may get people who are not customers, and you don't want that. You want people that you know have experience with your business and your services so that you can really get some details.

In this survey you're going to only ask them two questions. That's it.

Remember, make it easy for them. You're only asking two questions and these two questions should take them literally a minute or two to fill out. You're being respectful of their time and making it very easy for them to do.

When you're doing a survey you don't want to ask too much. You just want to get in, get the big picture - the big answers you want, and then get the heck out of there because the more you put in there, the less likely people are going to be inclined to give you input.

If you say, "Please help me fill out this short survey," and they click the link and it's 10+ questions long, there's a good chance they might say, "Ack, I don't have time for that many questions," and skip it.

Remember, they've got stuff to do. So if you make it any longer than they think is "quick", they're never going to do it.

Two questions is a no brainer though. Everyone can take a moment to answer two measly questions.

Here are the questions you're going to ask:

1. Please rate our services from 1 to 10 (1 being "you suck" and 10 being "awesome!!!!")

That's the simple question that's easy to answer. The second question is where the magic happens.

2. If your answer for question 1 was anything less than 10, what would it take to make it a 10?

Here you leave a spot where they can write as much as they like. It's simple but open ended so it encourages them to give some details. If they didn't think your services were the best they could possibly be - if they rated it a nine or less - they will be forced to think about it and tell you why it wasn't it perfect, which is what you're going to look to improve upon.

This is where your gold is.

It's super simple and very easy to answer these questions and you're going to quickly see how your customers really feel about your business. With that information, you have a plan for what you need to start fixing and/or improving.

EXPECTATIONS

When you're asking for surveys, you have to understand that most people are not going to fill it out - even if it's easy to do and would only take a minute. So you can't get offended that you sent this questionnaire to 500 of your customers and only 40 of them filled it out. I would actually be pretty happy about getting that many back.

You have to understand that, even though it's super simple, people still are not going to go out of their way for you because they are busy with their own stuff. Don't take it personally - just focus on the responses you get back.

Now, if you have a good relationship with your customers, they will be more motivated to fill it out, especially since it's super simple and easy. I recommend you send them to the survey via email. The email, just like the survey, should be short and sweet.

It should be friendly and just ask them for a quick favor. You say you're always trying to improve and they can help by just answering two short questions. It's important to let them know precisely how short is it so no matter where they are reading it, they

Survey Says . . .

know they can finish it quickly. You want them to fill it out the first time they open the email.

Then you give them the link and thank them. Easy stuff.

You tell them it's two questions in your email because you want them to know up front that it really is only going to take them two minutes. Otherwise they might think when they get over to the survey that it's actually 10 minutes of their time and they don't want to commit to that.

Keep your email short and to the point.

Here's an email I sent out to the students of my online dog trainer program:

Hi {first_name}.

I have a quick favor to ask . . .

Would you please fill out this super short (2 question) survey for me? It will take you literally 2 minutes to fill out and would really be helping me improve The FernDog Trainer Academy.

TAKE SURVEY

I am dedicated to your success and this info will enable me to make The Academy better for everyone, helping you be the best dog trainer you can be.

Thank you so much - I **REALLY** appreciate you doing this for me.

Have a great rest of the day!

Fern

Here are my stats after 24 hours for that email:

			46.3% OPENS	26.8% CLICKS
	FDTA survey I could really use your help	164 RECIPIENTS	76 OPENS	44 CLICKS

Considering that the average email open rate across all industries is less than 20% (shocking I know), I'm pretty happy with a 46.3% open in the first day. Of the 76 people who opened my email, 44 of them clicked over to go to the survey. Not a bad click through rate either.

Send it out and see what kind of responses you get. Then go through them and sort through the feedback people left you. Some of the stuff they mention you won't be able to do anything about, like if they want cheaper prices or something that's out of your realm of handling.

However, if 80 percent of them say you're too expensive, then you might want to look into your pricing options. The key is to look for common threads and what the majority thinks. You might see a common theme of customer service or that it takes too long to get their dog in and out of there. Look for those things, and whatever is really quick and easy, fix immediately and then make an action plan to work on any of the other comments that you think are really worthwhile.

If you see that a lot of people are commenting about a specific thing in your business - pay attention! Your customer base is the best market research you can do – think of them as your own personal quality control department.

Here are the survey results:

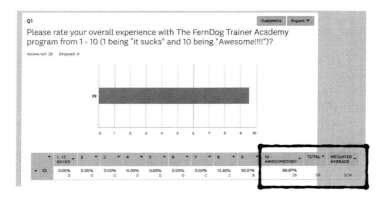

It seems I'm doing a pretty good job according to the responses I got. Twenty six of the thirty eight responders gave me a 10, eight gave me a 9, and five gave me an 8. I didn't receive anything lower than that.

From this sample I can see that I'm doing a nice job providing value to my students and keeping them happy. However, there is always room for improvement.

Looking into their responses I see that a few people request some more videos of me directly working with dogs and a couple wanted hands on training.

So my homework will be to turn those thirteen less than perfect ratings into 10's. I plan on hiring a video guy to follow me on a few interesting sessions and perhaps create a yearly live event (something I tried to do last year but didn't put enough effort into).

When your customers speak, listen.

You should keep doing this each and every year. The first time you do it, you're going to get a whole bunch of people that are going to say you aren't a 10. Again, don't take it personally, but look at it as an amazing opportunity. Then the next time you survey them, you'll do better because you've listened to them and implemented on the feedback they gave you the year before.

You'll keep improving and you're going to get to the point where you're consistently pinning the needle at 10 and that's an awesome place to be. You will know for sure that you're doing the very best for your customers and when your customers are rating you a 10, they're never going to go someplace else because there are no 11's .

ACTION PLAN

Go to surveymonkey.com and create your own 2 questions survey and send it to your customer list. Once you get the results, make any necessary adjustments to convert more people to a 10.

4

Magical Business Lessons From Disney

From the moment your kids are born you start thinking about your first trip to Walt Disney World. Whether you want to or not you'll find yourself there at least once before your kids hit their tenth birthday.

A few years ago, right after Thanksgiving, my family headed down to Orlando to make our second Disney pilgrimage. We had gone once before, when my girls were seven and I really pushed for this trip because I wanted to do it again while my kids still have some of that wide-eyed wonder.

I have to admit I was a bit excited myself. I'm just a big kid at heart and was as giddy as my kids to hit the Magic Kingdom and see that big mouse.

If you've been to Disney you know that this is no cheap trip - the cost was three times that of any vacation we've ever gone on (I had to sell some internal organs to make it happen – who needs a spleen anyway). So why did we, and millions of others, shell out all that cash when we could go to anywhere else for much less money?

The answer is simple. **No one does it like Disney**.

I'm kind of a Disney fanatic. Not the usual kind though.

I don't have Mickey Mouse figurines all over my house, Dumbo salt and pepper shakers or a large selection of mouse ears. Although I do love all that stuff, what most impresses me is Walt Disney himself and the amazing business he was able to create.

Businesses from all over the world actually study Disney to see how to run a company and create the very best customer experience. Countless books have been written about Walt and the business principals that have made the company a global powerhouse.

Walt Disney had to overcome huge obstacles to achieve all of his successes. It was only his sheer determination in the face of pretty extreme circumstances that he was able to persevere and keep his dream alive (when most people would have quit ten times over).

He really showed us that "all of our dreams can come true, if we have the courage to pursue them," (one of my favorite Walt quotes – I have this hanging in my office). Walt had such big dreams and some really amazing accomplishments, but at the same time, he had so many failures that would have crushed the normal person.

Walt was the master at creating exceptional products and services by making sure to always focus on the customer's experience. I've modeled so many of his business principals in my own business endeavors with great success and I am going to share some of them with you here.

The other thing exceptional about Walt is that, unlike some of the other great business innovators that we study (Steve Jobs comes to mind), Walt was a really good person as well. He was loved by those who worked for him he created a company culture second to none. So many of the people that worked for him stayed with him for decades and spoke so highly of him. He considered his staff family and even though he demanded such excellence out of them, he still treated them with love and he always took care of them.

I planned this latest trip to The Magic Kingdom at this time for two main reasons. One, the week after Thanksgiving is one of the quietest times in Disney so the lines would be at their shortest. And two, I would be there on my birthday (December 5th), which I just happen to share with my man Walt. After being so inspired by him, I thought it fitting that I would celebrate our birthday together in his magical world.

Although I promised myself I would unplug and not do any work during my Disney trip, my entrepreneurial mind is always working in the background with no known off switch. So as I spent my days and nights enjoying the Disney parks I couldn't help but notice some of the super cool things Disney does to create such raving fans that come back year after year.

Disney is really operating at the highest level of customer satisfaction and if you look at what Disney does and model it your business can see similar results. If you embrace and implement one or more of the following lessons, I guarantee your customers will be happier, your brand will become stronger and your business will thrive.

Here are just some of things that Disney does to make one of the best companies on the planet.

1 - Little details can make a big difference

By day two of my trip my family and I developed a golden rule of being in Disney: always look up. No matter where we were, on line for an attraction, in a gift shop, at a restaurant, you name it, there was always something cool in every nook and cranny – especially the ceilings. Every corner of the Disney parks are intricately designed which really adds to the wow factor and the impression visitors take away with them.

TAKEAWAY: Don't overlook or undervalue the little details of your product or service. Often it's those little, seemingly trivial details which will have your customers talking to their friends about your business.

2 - People will happily pay for convenience

Disney prides itself on their customer service and does everything it can to make your stay easy and enjoyable. We were staying at one of the Disney hotels which comes with some nice perks that make it well worth the cost.

One of the most annoying things about air travel is waiting for your luggage at the airport. Disney knows it's no fun so they do it for you. Once you land you skip baggage claim and go right to the Disney bus they have waiting for you (with comfy chairs, a TV and a bathroom – another big plus) and they get your bags and put them in your room. And they check your bags in (and do your boarding passes) for your return trip.

They even got us on a special expedited security line so we could get to our plane faster and easier (this was huge because the regular line to get through security was a mess). And Disney created their own bus line just to take guests right to their hotel at no extra cost.

These perks are things that are well worth any extra expense in my book and it was all included in our Disney package.

TAKEAWAY: If you find ways to make your customers lives easier and give them "VIP" treatment you'll be able to charge a premium for your services.

3 - Go all out (no matter what)

The day we went to Epcot Center it was kind of a slow day there. There weren't as many people as is normally there so the crowds were less and the lines were much shorter than usual. Great for us but not so great for Disney.

Every night they put on a huge water, fireworks and light show in the center of the small lake in the center of the park. It's really an amazing show and there's really no way I can describe it to do it justice. I can't imagine how much money and man power the show must take to pull off each night.

Did Disney cut it short or put less energy into it because the crowds were small? Hell no! They rocked it like the park was packed giving the people that were there an amazing show.

TAKEAWAY: I don't care how many customers you have, go all out every day and you'll see those crowds build over time.

4 - Offer complementary products and services

When you go to Disney there's lots of other stuff that you need throughout your stay. Disney knows this and instead of just letting you get it for yourself, they offer it all for you.

Knowing that the parks are huge and a day at any of the Disney properties require lots of walking (my wife wore a pedometer and we clocked in at 8 – 10 miles per day) Disney rents strollers for kids and motorized scooters for people with handicaps, for the elderly or those just plain lazy. They also sell food and drinks throughout each park.

Now you can get all those things yourself and bring them in but it's easier to just let Disney take care of the arrangements. They make your life easier and they make more money off each customer – a win/win.

TAKEAWAY: Look at your business and find some products or services that complement yours or are necessary for what you do and offer them to your customers for extra income streams.

5 - Position upsells and downsells at the right time

Disney is the master at this. The exits for all of their rides empty out into a gift shop that has items specific for that ride. You're all excited about the ride, in the prime state for buying so Disney leads you right to the sale.

In Animal Kingdom we went on a ride called the Kali River Rapids, where you sit in a raft and jet down some simulated rapids. The sign outside the ride says, "On this ride you will get wet and you might get soaked." So you would think people would be prepared to come off the ride drenched. Not so much.

After coming off the ride dripping wet we came out to a small gift shop selling shoes, towels and clothing. My wife bought a towel and sun dress so she didn't have to be wet and uncomfortable (I sucked it up wet, marveling at Disney's genius).

TAKEAWAY: If you position your additional offerings at just the right time, in just the right place, the sale is inevitable.

6 - Do things so good, so different or so big that you have no competition

Although there are other amusement parks like Busch Gardens and Sea World out there they can't even begin to compare to everything that Disney has to offer. All those other places don't have the quality and size of what Disney has.

People don't come back year after year to go to those places and none of the other parks have the brand recognition that Disney does. Disney is one of a kind and that's a really great position to be in as a business. The only real competition Disney has is themselves (Magic Kingdom, Epcot, Animal Kingdom, Hollywood Studios, Blizzard Beach, etc) – not bad at all.

TAKEAWAY: If you can do things so good, or so different or so big no one will ever be able to compete with you. Disney does all three.

7 - Create an experience worth talking about

Talk to someone coming home from a Disney vacation and you won't hear things like, "it was pretty good," or "I liked it." No, you'll hear things like, "It was amazing!" and "The best vacation of my life," and "You have to go there!"

When I got back and didn't wait for the topic of my vacation to come up to talk about it. No way! I was busting to tell everyone about the amazing time we had, fill them in on all the great details and insist that they get their butt's there as soon as possible.

<u>TAKEAWAY:</u> You don't want satisfied customers – that's the fastest way to mediocrity (and that sucks). You want to create raving fans that will be telling everyone they bump into about your business. To do that you need to give them an experience that's worth talking about. Something special that separates you from the rest and leaves them with a big, fat smile on their face. It doesn't have to be big or expensive, it just has to be memorable.

8 - Always keep improving and innovating

Walt Disney World opened in October of 1971 and has been a monstrous success pretty much ever since that first day. So with a successful product you would think that Disney would just keep everything as is. Why mess with a proven winner?

Disney understands that to have long lasting success you need to constantly strive to make things better. Every single year Disney rolls out new rides and makes improvements and innovations to all of their parks. Although some of their popular attractions have been left pretty much as is, the parks are always evolving.

Walt was known to always say to his staff, "How can we plus it?"

When they worked hard and created an amazing movie or attraction, Walt always wanted to take it up to an even higher level. Then, he would "plus the plus."

TAKEAWAY: Even if you have a successful product and service think about how you can make it better. How can you improve all the things you do each and every year? Strive to keep everything you do current with the times and utilize the latest technology where appropriate.

9 - Pay attention to what your customers do

When we purchased our Disney vacation package we each got our very own MagicBand, which is a bracelet that acts as our room key, entry into the parks and contains all of our package details, credit card info and identification. At first I thought this was just a cool convenience but then realized that it's an amazing tool for Disney to do valuable market research.

We wore the bands every day, everywhere and used them to get on each ride, to pay for things in the gift shops, for any food and to access our hotel room. Because of this Disney knows exactly where I went and what I purchased, and can use this information to send me specific offers in the future based on what they know I like and to see what's popular with different demographics.

<u>TAKEAWAY:</u> Make sure you pay attention to what your customers do, what they buy and how they buy it from you. Then, tailor your messages, sales offers and customer services to the specific behavior of each customer. This will really make your customer feel connected to you and help you know what you need to focus on for future customers.

10 - Forming partnerships to expand your reach

In Hollywood Studios you'll find The Rock 'n Roll Roller Coaster Starring Aerosmith. Unfortunately my kids are still a bit too small to go on this high octane roller coaster but that didn't stop me from checking it out by myself while my family spent some more money in one of the gazillion gift shops.

The coaster was fast – real fast. I mean crazy fast. The ride was fun but I was more impressed with what Disney did here with this roller coaster. By partnering up with a popular rock band they are bringing in a whole host of fans that might never be interested in coming to check out the park otherwise.

Aerosmith fans will want to be a part of anything the band is involved with and will want to check out the ride and in turn Hollywood Studios, exposing the park to customers they might not have been able to reach on their own. I'm sure Aerosmith also did some promoting of it when it first opened giving Disney free publicity.

TAKEAWAY: Find some businesses that share your target customers and find a way to partner with them and you'll get a whole new audience, spreading your brand farther. Just make sure that the partnership is beneficial for both parties so

11 - Turn downside into upsides

One of the most annoying things about going to Walt Disney World is waiting in all those lines. The Seven Dwarves Mine Train in The Magic Kingdom park is only a few years old and one of the most popular rides there. Lines while I was there ranged anywhere from 60 to 120 minutes long on average. That's a long time to wait for a little roller coaster that only lasts a few minutes.

Disney knows this is a pain point for everyone so they decided to turn the process of waiting on line into a fun experience. On the line as you're waiting for the ride Disney put in all kinds of interactive games and displays for the kids to do to keep them happily busy while they wait on line.

We had a Fast Pass for the ride (which means we got to skip the line and go right to the front) but my kids wanted to go back – not because of the ride but because they wanted to wait in line and do all the fun activities during the wait. Well done Disney.

TAKEAWAY: What are some things about your business that are a bit of a bummer for your customers? Think up ways you can turn them around and make them either a positive or minimize the negative as much as you can. How can you enhance your client's experience – especially in the areas before or after they are using your service?

It could be something like free coffee in your lobby or a special bonus if your boarding services are booked up for the weekend and customers can't get in. Be creative and experiment a bit to find the best fit for each situation.

12 - Find out what your customers think

Walt was known for disguising himself, going undercover and seeing things from his customer's perspective. He would constantly go through the rides and attractions, not as the boss, but as a customer. He would experience it from an outside perspective so he can better understand how it made the customers feel.

He would also walk up to people and talk to them, asking them what they liked and what they didn't like. This gave him unbiased golden nuggets about how he could improve things.

My last dog, Hayley, was not a daycare kind of dog so I never used daycare with her. Even though I worked at a few dog daycares and now consult at daycares all over the country, it wasn't until I got my new puppy and become a customer of daycares that I really saw how different that perspective is.

Using these same facilities as a customer exposed strong and weak points in the businesses that I wasn't aware of on the other side.

<u>TAKEAWAY</u>: You need to get the customer's point of view on how your business works and use that information to improve it. Pick a friend to go through your services (without alerting your staff) and report back to what they liked and what might need improvement.

You should also survey your customers at least once a year to see how you're doing and find places you can improve. Always be improving! I do it every year and it always gives me great feedback on how I can improve my business.

13 - Dream big

Walt Disney said, "I only hope that we never lose sight of one thing – that it was all started by a mouse."

He definitely had no idea that sketching out a simple cartoon mouse would grow into one of the biggest businesses in the world, but that's how it all began. Walt first conceived of Mickey Mouse on a long train ride at a time when his business was failing.

Even though at the time it looked like Walt's business was headed for disaster he had a vision and a belief that big things were ahead. He never stopped thinking big and after every setback he took a new (seemingly small) step forward again.

TAKEAWAY: Set big goals, dream big and don't let obstacles stop you. Just find a new direction to go in or a new action to take and remember these words from the late, great Walt Disney, *"What ever you do, do it well. Do it so well that when people see you do it they will want to come back and see you do it again and they will want to bring others and show them how well you do what you do."*

5

Stealing Customers From Your Competition

Something kind of strange happened to me in my dog training business.

I got a voice mail from a woman named Nikki saying she has a puppy and wanted to schedule in some training. That's not the strange part, I get calls like this all the time.

The strange part happened when I called her back. Nikki explained that she had reached out to me before she had gotten her puppy and that she had worked with another trainer a few weeks ago. This was not completely unusual, I often get clients who were not happy with another trainer they worked with.

As I always do when I hear they've worked with someone else, I asked why they didn't continue working with the other trainer. I want to find out what they worked on and why they weren't satisfied with so that I'm not repeating things that didn't work or they don't like. This is where it got strange.

Nikki informed me that they liked the other trainer. She went over stuff with them and they were seeing results because of it. They liked her, yet didn't want her back – or more specifically they would rather work with me. Why?

It doesn't make much sense and I was a bit confused until Nikki continued. She said she had been watching some of my videos and really liked them so she decided to have me come in instead of the other trainer.

Do you understand how amazing that is?

Satisfied customers rarely look to other businesses because their needs are being met. However, Nikki dropped her first trainer not because she messed up and not because I solicited her – she came to me.

No More Mild Mannered Business

Here's what I think happened. Nikki called and spoke with a bunch of trainers and then chose one that was probably a little less expensive than I am. She did the session and was happy with the trainer. Then something happened. I popped up again. Either on social media or in an email or just searching on the internet for more info. She was watching a video or two of me and decided that I kind of know what I'm talking about, or maybe she was amused by my funny banter. Either way, the video (or videos – or maybe some other contributing content) convinced her to leave the trainer she liked and pay more for me, who she now perceived as a better option.

I didn't do anything – she came right to me. And she booked a 4 session package with me before I even met her. She went from thinking I was too expensive to leaving someone she liked to pay me much more money. My sneaky secret weapon to accomplish this amazing feat is simple content. I just created some videos that provided value and let her get to know me, while positioning me as an expert.

The even cooler thing is I haven't done any new videos in a while so it's very likely I made them years ago . . . and they are still working for me.

I hope you appreciate and grasp the magnitude of this concept. I'm able to steal away my competition's customers EVEN IF THEY ARE HAPPY WITH THEM. And I don't even have to try – she came to me.

Cool, or what?!

This is the power of creating content. It indoctrinates people to your brand, provides value up front, positions you as the expert and keeps you top of mind. I guarantee you that businesses who produce content will always win over their competitors, all other things being equal.

One of my recent business coaches calls content assets. Once created, they work for you and you can leverage them any time in the future. I really like that association. Creating content doesn't have to be a one and done kind of thing – it can live on and work for you, ongoing.

Video is hands down the best way to create the most personal connection with your audience. I don't think my new client, Nikki would have bailed on her first trainer if I only had blog posts out there. It was my videos that sold her on me.

Now I don't know if the other trainer was putting out any kind of content – actually I do kind of know, and she wasn't. How can I be so sure? Easy, there are no other trainers in my area who are doing what I do with content.

Not because they can't, they can. Anyone can shoot some videos and put them online. Hell, most teenagers do it but not most businesses. And that's my big competitive advantage. I'll do what they won't do. I'll take the time to learn how to do it and I'll risk looking stupid on camera (which happens all the time by the way), when everyone else won't do those things.

This is a HUGE opportunity for you as well. Look at the other businesses in your area. Are any of them putting out video content on a regular basis? I'm guessing no. Very few businesses in any industry really do it. Not because it's readily available and easy to do, but because they don't want to put the effort in.

It's a choice. I choose to do these things because I understand the big picture. Short-sighted businesses only think about the time it will take then to do it right now. All my videos are still working for me – even those I created ten years ago. Always keep the big picture in mind.

Here are 2 easy-peasy video ideas that you can immediately start doing to build your assets and get this video mojo working for you:

ACTION PLAN

1. Customer case study. Spotlight a customer that has gotten some great results using your service. Show how they were able to overcome their obstacles and celebrate their new success.

2. A Video blog. Do behind the scenes videos showing what goes on in your business on a day to day basis. This lets everyone get to know you and see the stuff you do, warming them up and moving closer to the sale.

Remember, he who creates the most assets in their business usually wins. Will it be you?

6

Dealing with Dick

No matter what you do, you're going to put up with unhappy and/or unreasonable customers every now and then. In the many years of my dog training business I've only had to deal with a handful of unsatisfied customers. If you're good at what you do and take pride in helping your customers, it usually works out that way.

But even if you do everything right, you're still going to come across the occasional pain in the ass. A few years back I had one such experience in my dog training business.

It's all because of an email I got from a client that I did a private session with. I'm always so excited to see an email from a client because I love to hear how I've impacted their life and learn about the difference I made with their dog.

This email, however, was not that kind of email. It was actually the other kind. The kind that we never like to get and, thankfully, are extremely rare.

The email started like this:

> Hi Fernando,
>
> I have to say we were upset and disappointed with our consultation yesterday. The more I've thought about it, the more upset I've become about it because plain and simple I feel that nothing was accomplished...

It took me completely by surprise because they didn't say anything to me during the session that would lead to be believe they were unhappy and (thankfully) this was the very first negative email I've ever received from a client as a dog trainer.

The Session

My client, who we'll just call Richard – Dick for short, and his wife were referred to me by another dog trainer in the area who's a friend of mine. I spoke with Dick's wife on the phone and she told me they just adopted a dog two months ago and have seen some separation anxiety and some pretty intense leash reactivity for no apparent reason. And she said they also want to just make sure they're doing everything right. I told them how I work and what my fee was. They agreed and we set the appointment for Sunday afternoon.

During the beginning of the session we discussed their dog's separation anxiety which I would consider mild. Then I learned that Dick's last dog had suffered from severe separation anxiety, and after some questioning it becomes obvious that Dick was a contributing factor to the anxiety. I then went over how they can treat the separation anxiety with their new dog so she doesn't go down the same path as the last dog.

It's at this point I notice Dick starting to pout and I'm not really sure why or what to do about it (now I realize that it's probably because I implied – in a nice way – that he contributed to his last dog's anxiety and his ego was bruised) but I figure if he had a problem he would tell me like an adult instead of pouting like a child.

The session goes on with me focusing on the things that I see as important: separation anxiety, their relationship and communication with the dog, and the reactivity on leash (which I never saw because the dog did awesome outside when we took her for a walk). At the end of the session they wrote me a check, smiled, shook my hand and I left.

The Email

In his email after our session, Dick went on to tell me that he's a "physician and someone that has had dogs all his life and studied comparative physiology in college," which tells me he's kind of full of himself (what does being a doctor have to do with anything?) and a bit of a know it all. Then Dick goes into how they just wanted me to teach come, down and to give paw instead of wasting their time on my theories on behavior.

Never during our initial phone conversations did they say they wanted me to teach obedience or tricks and only at the very end of our session did they mention it in passing.

The last thing Dick's email said was that he thought I was overpriced (they agreed to my fee before I went there) and wanted some or all of his money back.

Handling It

Dick's email made me more than a little pissed off.

I spent 2 hours of my time on a Sunday to go over the issues that can greatly impact their life with their dog. They hired me as an expert to give them advice. They agreed to pay my fee.

They say the customer is always right, but I don't buy that. Is Dick right here? Does he deserve his money back?

Personally, I don't believe that "the customer is always right." In fact, sometimes, the customer is very wrong – and sometimes the customer is a Dick. They agreed on my pricing beforehand and I provided the services I was hired for, so giving him any or all of his money back is the same as him stealing from me.

So what did I do? What would you do?

I know what I wanted to do . . . but instead I gave him his money back.

My first response was to be angry and very defensive. I was extremely tempted to immediately write him back and say everything that I just said above.

However, that would be a mistake. That would lead me to write an emotionally charged email and make me just like Dick. I'm better than that and what would that actually accomplish?

So instead I took some time to cool down and think about it, which is something I strongly encourage you do if you find yourself in a similar situation. You don't want to immediately respond and say stuff in a bad state of mind. Instead, settle down and think rationally, not emotionally.

On the next page you can see my email back to him:

No More Mild Mannered Business

> Hi Dick.
>
> I'm sorry you didn't like our session.
>
> For me, the important thing (and what my job is) is to look into your situation and pick the important things to focus on. And that is the reactivity on leash and unexplained reactions outdoors. That could become a major issue if not identified and addressed. I also want to make sure you are setting yourself up to have a happy, healthy dog long term – and obedience and tricks are nice but won't have the biggest impact on your dog's behavior.
>
> Although I don't give refunds because my service is my time and I'm blessed enough to be very busy right now, I don't want your money if you feel my time wasn't worth anything to you. So I'm ripping up your check and you don't have to pay me at all.
>
> I wish you all the best.
>
> Fern

That's not the email I wanted to write but it's the one I had to write.

There's obviously no talking rationally to someone who's irrational – nothing good will come of it. So the best course of action was to give him his money back and be done with him forever.

Don't get me wrong, I hated doing it and I really needed that money. But like everything else in running a business, you have to think big picture.

Knowing I gave him his money back will probably be enough to let him go back to his pouting in private. However, if I was confrontational and argued with him, there's a chance that he might go out of his way to bad mouth me in public, which could negatively affect my business in worse ways. Even though he's in the wrong, it really doesn't matter – the damage will still be done.

In my opinion, the money I lost was well worth never having to ever see Dick again, so I can get back to my true clients, who appreciate me and what I do. I've already given Dick too much of my time and energy and don't what to give him any more.

It's not perfect but I think it's the best way to handle situations like this. It's not about right or wrong and it's never personal – I actually did a great session and this is in no way a reflection of my abilities. It's just about doing what's best for your business and not dwelling on the Dicks of the world.

7

The Dangers of Bad Customers Service

Are you aware of the massive ripple effect that your customer service is causing?

It's one of the most important things small businesses need to understand if they are going to be around in a couple years. And I'm pretty sure you do want your business not only around, but to be successful.

Okay, listen up and learn from a recent experience I had that is a perfect example of how a lazy, short-sighted, poorly managed and/or uncaring business really shot themselves in the foot. And if they repeat this (which I'm sure they will), their business will find itself spiraling downward.

Apathy on Skates

My wife and I wanted our twin seven-year-old daughters to do some kind of physical activity to keep them active and have some fun. They didn't really like playing soccer or have any desire to do any other team sport, so when they said they wanted to try skating, we thought it might be a perfect fit for them.

So we signed them up at a local ice rink for seven lessons to see if they liked skating. If they did, we would continue to send them for as long as they wanted to go (possibly into young adulthood).

Almost immediately it became obvious to me that their instructor was horrible. She showed very little interest in actually interacting with the kids and clearly did the bare minimum to get her paycheck. Even to a novice skater like myself, it was clear that she was doing next to nothing and my girls who hit the ice face-first often, as well as the other kids, were struggling because of her lack of involvement.

My one daughter summed it up perfectly when she said to me that the instructor just "told them what to do instead of teaching them."

During the second lesson I was forced to ask the instructor to go help my kids instead of just watching them repeatedly fall. Then after our fifth lesson I spoke with the skating director and told her (in a very nice and non-confrontational way) about how disappointed I was and detailed what I observed with the instructor.

She nodded halfheartedly and said she would look into it, but there was no change in the level of instruction (in fact it actually seemed to get even worse) and she didn't follow up with me at all. Disappointed and frustrated, we left after our seventh and final lesson never to return.

The Loss of One Customer

So what did the ice rink lose by losing my business?

Well, the lessons cost us $151 for the seven lessons including skate rentals, but you have to double that because I have two kids. So that's $302.

However, that's not what they lost. That's what they got from me as a one-time customer. Even though I thought the lessons sucked, my kids still actually really like ice skating and want to continue. If they did a good job with lessons (or at least an average job, or even addressed my concerns) we would have kept them in at least until summer.

That would have been $417 (two semesters at $151 and one at $115), times two girls, which comes out to $834.

We probably would've taken the summer off, but if they were still fired up about skating in the fall, we'd put them back in. I know it's impossible to predict how much they would have netted from us this year, but it would have at least been $834. And could have been as much as $3,336 per year.

And if my girls take a real liking to the sport and want to pursue it long-term, that would have meant about $16,680 if they took lessons until age 12. And it would be very possible that they would continue it well into their adulthood.

And that is for lessons only. They would most likely get additional income from us coming to do some family free skating, having their birthday party there (which they have already asked about), the girls going for some extra ice time, or buying skates and any other supplies. With all that added in they could have gotten over $20,000 - $25,000 from us over the next 5 - 10 years.

So, was it worth it for them to provide a crappy customer experience? Would that amount make a difference to your business?

You must always be thinking about the big picture and be very aware of the **lifetime value** of a customer. If the skating director did the math I bet she would have tried to be more helpful or at least made me feel like they really cared about how I felt. But she didn't and they lost me and my business.

Not providing a great customer experience only happens because of ignorance or laziness.

But that's not all - it gets worse for them.

What You Don't Know CAN Hurt You

What the ice rink (and many small businesses) don't realize is that it's so much easier and less expensive to address my concerns and make me happy than to go out and find a new customer. According to the White House Office of Consumer Affairs, loyal customers are worth 10 times as much as their first purchase.

That's huge, my friend. Especially when you understand that you have approximately a 5 - 20% chance of selling to a new prospect, but a **60 -70% probability of selling to an existing customer**. Clearly it's so much easier to sell to someone who's already in the door than to go out and hustle to find someone new and convince them to become a buyer.

What it boils down to is that it is 6 - 7 times more expensive (and exhausting) to acquire a new customer than to keep a current one (also according to White House Office of Consumer Affairs.) So you must, Must, **MUST** take care of the customers you have.

I want you to stamp that on your brain and make sure you operate your business with this in mind. Otherwise you'll be working your ass off but going nowhere (sound familiar? - we've all been there).

Put most of your time and energy into listening and taking care of the customers you have right now. I would say somewhere around 6 - 7 times more time, energy and money go into your existing customer base.

Now you can see that the ice rink is losing so much more than that $25,000 lifetime customer value because they now have to go out and spend the cash to get someone new to come in their doors. But their monetary loss is about to get much worse.

I'll get to that in a minute, but first we need to look at why they should have been overjoyed that I was unhappy.

Listen To Your Customers

Get this; <u>a typical business only hears from 4% of their dissatisfied customers</u>. That's it, 4%. So the overwhelming majority of people who are not happy with what you and your business are providing are quietly stewing and secretly plotting never to do business with you again.

So by taking the time to go out of my way to voice my concerns (and remember, I wasn't nasty about it, I just told them how I honestly felt), I was pointing out something that could be present in the minds of many other dissatisfied customers.

I was showing them how they could make their business better – for free. Instead of seeing me as a pest, they should have used my conversation with the skating director as valuable market research and then used that information to create a better business.

Now, not all complaints are going to warrant action, but all customers should feel heard. And even if you don't change what you're doing, you should at least make that customer feel like you care about his opinion.

So don't get defensive when a customer complains. Actively listen to what they are telling you and then go back and honestly assess your business and see if you need to fix some things – odds are you do.

The good news is that you don't have to wait until someone complains. You can survey your customers to see what they really think right now. With a simple tool like Survey Monkey, you can set up a short survey to email your customers, which they can fill out anonymously and give you a window into what they really think.

It's a good practice to send a short (3 - 8 question) survey to your customer base at least once a year to see how you can better serve them. That way you can make sure you keep them and save all that cash it would cost you to acquire new customers.

When your customers talk, listen. Customer complaints are actually golden nuggets of how to improve your business.

Now let's see how the ice rink's loses get so much worse.

Social Media Aftermath

So far we've just looked at the long-term loss of losing one customer. However, the ripple of effects of my poor experience at the ice rink has only just begun.

I didn't let it end with me walking out of the rink after my kids' last skating lesson. Not only were my concerns not addressed, the last lesson was by far the worst of the bunch. The instructor took her lack of interest to a new level, and with every minute that went by during that last lesson, I got more and more pissed off.

Five years ago it wouldn't have made that much of a difference for the ice rink. At worst, I could have complained to the other parents around me at the rink and told my immediate friends over the next week or so as I spoke to them. But in today's age of technology, I have so much more power and ability to impact the ice rink's bottom line.

I was so unhappy with what I saw, watching my kids basically teach themselves how to skate, that I couldn't wait another second to tell the world what a bad job the ice rink was doing. So I pulled my special worldwide communicator out of my pocket (aka iPhone) and angrily pecked out a Facebook post detailing my unhappiness and warning everyone else to stay away.

It took me about five minutes, and I even included a picture of the instructor leaning against the wall while my kids were all the way on the far side of the rink (the image shows my one daughter face down on the ice too). It was so simple and easy to do.

Within minutes I had a whole bunch of comments from friends who live right in the area thanking me for letting them know. Two of them even said they were considering going there but now would not waste their time or money. Some people even commented with other competing ice rinks that we could use.

So let's just say that, because of my post, two people will now never go to that ice rink and will bring their business to the competition. So the ice rink lost out on my lifetime value ($20,000 - $25,000) and now possibly an additional two more lifetime values. So now their losses have moved up to around $60,000 lifetime (assuming that each person has 2 kids, which my friends did).

Even if we wouldn't have been customers for years, they still just threw at least a few hundred dollars away. And don't forget, I'm just one person. If you only know of 4% of your dissatisfied customers, how many other parents had the same experience and went to social media to vent?

The average Facebook user has about 350 friends and the average Twitter user has about 208 followers. So now the "average" person has the ability to influence quite a few people. And that's just the average. The ice rink might be interested to know that I have over 4,400 Facebook "friends" which means the ripple effect can go so much farther.

Social media is a game changer for businesses. And those that understand its implications and how to harness its power will succeed, while those that don't will find themselves bleeding money.

I was able to immediately report how I was feeling and influence the buying decisions of everyone in my circle of influence. Then those people can also share my experience with their network and a domino effect of bad press can ensue.

That's pretty bad news for the ice rink, but I didn't let it end there.

I was so dissatisfied with the lessons that later that night I logged onto Yelp, the online business rating website, and left them a one star review and detailed all the ways they let me down. Yelp.com gets 178 million unique visitors each month. That's a lot of eyeballs and personal reviews are one of the top ways that people make buying decisions.

So, how many customers did the ice rink lose by providing a bad service and doing a horrible job of addressing a customer who told them they were not satisfied? I would say they lost out big time. And if they continue this way, they will find themselves out of business in the very near future.

An Incredible Opportunity For Your Business

Businesses like the ice rink are providing the rest of us with an amazing opportunity. They are making it so easy for good companies who care about providing a great product and service to shine and thrive.

The door is wide open for you to create a customer experience that is so good that you will have zero competition and people will happily pay you more because of it. In fact, a whopping 90% of U.S. Consumers say they would pay more for a better customer experience (according to Customer Experience Impact Report by Harris Interactive/RightNow, 2010). You can charge more for your product or service and do nothing but make sure you're providing a great experience for your customers. Sounds like a no brainer to me.

The bottom line here is that you cannot risk doing a crappy job or being lazy with your customer service. Consumers will not tolerate it, and today, they have the power to directly influence your revenue. **It's time to step it up** and fill the gap that consumers are craving.

The Dangers Of Bad Customers Service

Keep improving what you do, listen to your customers, be proactive with any concerns and don't piss your customers off by not making them feel heard and cared for.

Organic vs. Paid

Are you hungry?

Let's pretend you are and that it's getting close to lunch time, so you start thinking about what to eat. Let's say you're trying to be healthy and decide that even though a greasy burger and french fries sounds perfect, a salad would be a much smarter choice.

Now you could go to the store and buy some seeds, come home, plant them in your back yard, water them, keep the animals and bugs away, cultivate them as they grow and finally, months later you get to pick all those veggies, wash them up and then prepare them into your salad.

Organic Vs. Paid

You could do it that way – and some people do. It's very cheap to do it this way because all you really need to pay for is the seeds. So, do you get your lunch this way?

No, of course not. The problem is that you're hungry NOW, not it a couple of months and ever since the supermarket was invented you get to skip all that work and just walk in and pay a small price to get your lunch and eat it right now, without wait and all that effort.

I'm going to go way out on a limb and say that you're not a farmer and get your lunch from the store. Most of us would starve, trying to grow our own food.

Sadly, I see so many people starving their business unnecessarily while there is a much easier option available sitting right there. It's called paid advertising and it's your ticket to filling your business's belly right now.

Trying to hustle with organic posting on social media, going to networking events, passing out flyers and waiting on word of mouth can bring in new customers, but at a snails pace and you need to ask yourself can you afford to wait. If you're hungry now, lunch in a few months is useless.

The good news is there is a top of the line supermarket for your business available where you can go in and for a few bucks get right in front of your ideal customers right now. It's called Facebook and Instagram and Google. These platforms are filled to the brim with exactly what your business needs and all you have to do is walk in, pay a little money and walk out with customers RIGHT NOW!

I'm not saying you need to abandon all your organic marketing efforts. Just like my friends who have gardens in the back yard to occasionally make some food for their family, you can still do the organic stuff in addition to your paid marketing. Just remember, all those people who have a garden use the store for 90% of their food. The gardens are just a supplement.

The problem that everyone runs into is that anyone can walk into a supermarket and easily find what they need and come out a winner. Online advertising is a bit more complex than that. It takes understanding how each platform works and knowing how to create an offer that appeals to your target market and to deliver it in a way that they prefer.

This is an amazing time in history. Thanks to technology, small businesses have access to the same powerful tools that the big brands use. High converting advertising used to only be realistic to huge companies with big budgets and resources. It required a team of people and a big bank roll to implement, manage and make convert.

Not anymore. Thanks to this glorious thing called the internet, the playing field has been leveled and we can now do the same things that large companies can do. We have access to the same tools and can make them work on any budget. Never before has this been possible. You are living in the single best time in human history to have a business.

At this moment Facebook (and Instagram, which is owned by Facebook) is both the most powerful and most affordable of all the advertising platforms available. It's where everyone is where all they eyeballs are – as of early 2019, 2.3 billion people are on Facebook. That's about 1/3 of planet Earth!

Not only is Facebook where everyone is hanging out, but because of all of the points of data Facebook collects they know so much about each of those people, so it's easy to only target the specific people who are most likely to be your ideal customers. This enables you to only spend money on showing your ads to those that are interested in what you're selling, making your costs go way down as opposed to traditional marketing methods (like coupon books, newspaper and magazine ads, and TV spots).

I also like Facebook over Google because for Google ads to work someone has to be actively searching for your solution online – they need to come to you. On Facebook, we don't have to wait for them to find us, we can go out and proactively get in front of them. And we can do it in a place they are familiar with and trust.

Even though it's so cost effective and so powerful, currently only 1% of businesses are utilizing it.

That's unbelievable. Here we have something that gives us the power to greatly speed up the process that we acquire customers and so few are taking advantage of this.

Organic Vs. Paid

I believe the main reason is because there are a lot of moving parts that go into running an ad campaign on social media, combined with it requires a fair amount of technical know how (Facebook definitely doesn't make it easy). The overwhelm of researching and creating the targeting audiences, coming up with images and videos that convert, writing effective copy, staying compliant with the rules and regulations, as well as the logistics of setting everything up and then monitoring it daily.

It's a lot.

I know because years ago when I first found out about Facebook ads I jumped in, placed a bunch of ads, blew through $500 and got no results. I was pissed off because I saw all these other businesses using Facebook ad successfully but it didn't work for me.

So I gave up.

For about a week I lost sleep over this. I thought to myself, "I'm a smart guy. If all these other people can figure it out, I should be able to as well."

Then it hit me. It's not that I was dumb or that it just couldn't work for me, it was that I just didn't know what I was doing. I just threw some ads up there without learning how to do it the right way. If others had figured it out, I just needed to find someone who knew what they were doing and have them teach me.

So that's what I did. I found a mentor, joined his coaching program and BAM! - my ads started working.

Since then, I've spend thousands of dollars on coaching and educating myself on the ins and outs of running successful ads on Facebook and Instagram. This has helped me grow my businesses, spread my message and make more money.

This barrier between all those great businesses that want and need to get more customers, and the Facebook (and Instagram) advertising platform is why I created my digital marketing agency. I want to let you utilize my education, experience and resources so that you can join the 1% and take your business from mild mannered to super-dooper!

The thing to remember is that this prosperous time for advertising on Facebook may not last. As more people start figuring out how to use it effectively,

Organic Vs. Paid

ad costs will go up as available advertising space on the platform gets filled up. The opportunity is there for those who are willing to take advantage of it.

My advice is to start using Facebook and Instagram ads right now and see what they can do for you. Another great thing about them is that you can set any budget and see results in real time, so you don't blow a big chuck of money.

If you really want to try it and realize that you need help (or have better things in your business to spend your time on), I would love to help you out. Just reach out to me at *fern@fjc-enterprises.com* and we can set up a time to talk and see if my services would be a good fit for your businesses.

Whatever you do, you need to be smart about how you're going to spend your time and money, while maximizing your results and moving your businesses in the right direction.

In Closing

Okay, you've read this entire little book. The question now is what are you going to do with all this information.

Will it just sit in your head as something that you'll get to "some day?"

Or will you take action and make it happen?

The choice is all yours. Statistics tell us that most people will do nothing and continue to do what they've always done – getting the results they've always gotten.

But a few of you will get a fire lit under you, you'll implement and see some results. You'll get inspired by this and double your efforts and before you

In Closing

know it you'll have blasted way past mild mannered and stepped into being a business superhero.

Up, up and away!

Looking for your very own Facebook/Instagram advertising hero?

Helping businesses get more leads and customers on these platforms is my specialty.

Get details and contact me over at
FJC-ENTERPRISES.COM

Made in the
USA
Columbia, SC

81110432R00063